# IN PERSON, ....

By
ANDREW ROBINSON

The Hovel Press 2022

## In Personam

Some of these poems have appeared in  magazines or pam-
phlets, including  Poetry on the  Lake, Poetry Cornwall,  and
ephemeral FPG and other writing group materials

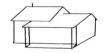

www.hovelpress.co.uk

carvoza@gmail.com

To the onlie begetters of these verses, Thank you:
You know where the bodies are buried.


With  thanks and appreciation to FPG

# The Poems

IN PERSONAM

## THIS IS A POEM

You read it because that's what poems are,
things to be read, or if not (read, that is,
for yourself) then listened to. You've got this far,
made a good start. *I don't understand Poetry*'s
a common excuse. Well, here's a thing,
neither do I. All I ever do is
try to tell the truth, which comes in a certain
rhythm. What some people call a voice.
It really is this simple. A poem
doesn't have to speak you off your feet,
take your breath away, or impress you
with rhetoric & artistry. The best
poems conceal the art and hard work
that goes into making them. Like this.

## AT THE BEACH

I used to sit at the beach with my Sister
and Mummy & Daddy and our other
sister, watching yachts on the near horizon
heel right over so their white, triangular
sails changed shape, and my Sister (she was bigger,
and knew almost everything then)
explained they were going ever so faster
because the sun was blue and the sea shone.
And along the far horizon daddy-ships
bent about their black, disappearing business.

Teenagers, we'd go sailing to see Daddy
or go to see Daddy who was sailing.
All we could do was do as we were told,
jump to working the boat about its burden
which he was in charge of and was always right.

One day we sailed along the coast, the yacht
heeling right over as if we were going
faster but the boom snagged in the salt water.
The sea was blue and the sun shone, looking
sharp at the beach too far away for children.

## In Truro Cathedral

Some days at the back of the church,
I sit by myself for a few minutes
in the reserved, memorial chapel
by the book of names in its cabinet.
I watch the shades & the coloured shadows
of the stained-glass windows into heaven;
look at the painting where Christ stands,
arms outstretched as if to bless, his feet
nailed to a corner of the round earth,
flanked by angels with impossible wings;
and if I could pray, I would. I think of you.
I shut my eyes, to meet the pulse of
retinal blood, reflected off the back
of my own closed eyelids. And in that streaming
dark, it's as if we were under water,
or meeting in a dream. Here's you,
with your greenie-blue-grey eyes
gazing out of silence into mine.
It might not sound like much but it's the best
we can do, the closest we get, for me to
sit by your name so blackly in the book.
Under glass. At the back of the church.

## APRON STRINGS

The children, rather than be taken
into care on the death of their mother
in default of other arrangements
were brought up by their father as a sole
parent having custody, care & control.
After the pitiful small-box funeral,
the trial, the inquest, the judicial
enquiry this, below, can be published.
If not to bring closure then in hope
of casting light on a chapter so dark
that any sane, right-thinking mind would
find it inexplicable, dispossessed
entirely of all rationality.
Among his papers, when they came to
put him away, going through everything,
looking for motive, hoping to research
some explanation, they found in a locked box
the lines here following, transcribed without
interpretation, editorial
matter, gloss, or comment:

## RE: MY CHILDREN

I have been your mother,
taught you how to make it through the day
and, how to find, meet, and recognize
a friend, companion, ally, fellow foot
soldier, lover. How to balance the 'I'
with the vision & parallax of 'We
can do this together', or, more exactly,
'I believe I can with you beside me–
How about it? what do you believe?'
And I have been your mother, pushing you out,
not 'born again', not 'once more entering'
but for the first time in the big wide world;
I have done all these things. And now
I can be me, and all the more (with what
you have taught me, and left me) be the 'me'
I was not born to be but have become.
I have learned how to deal with children,
how to catch them, keep them, fatten them up.
I have learned how to act the part
of the parent, how to cut the apron-strings,
so little feet can finally paddle off.
It's time for me, and, second time around
who says I have to be, what comforting
law of the universe is there that says
I have to be particularly nice?

## Recovery Visit

Today I went with our son to visit
my wife. He suggested we turn
out of our track to where we knew she was.
We had to check the map though, it was
so long since, and he told me he had
once before in his travels come here
with one of his sisters, and I too
had some years earlier visited
with her when we had similarly
turned to this same patch their mother holds
in quiet now enjoyment of her own.
Not that when I knew her she was one
to lie still, always on the go, she
kept me on my toes, life with her
was never dull, she always had some novel
and exciting purpose, some passionate
escapade, or some as here
overwhelming commitment.
Now my son and I speak with his mother
and of her, how she was and is, what it was like
what happened, and what it is like now,
she's cured of all her troubles twenty years.

## THE SLEEPERS

You are gone and there's nothing to say
nothing to be done or I can do
other than sit staring into space
or looking blankly at this blank sheet.
I'd write but you'd never read it
even if it tracked through. You never check
messages or mail. It's like home video
framing the dead, or captured footage
of the children. Words don't work any more
in the face of such absence. Cattle trucks
clank past one by one until each one
clanks past one by one until each one
is past with its freight, and all we're left with's
lines of infinitely distant sleepers.

## PRIMROSE

When first we met she was already
established in the congregation.
She would sit firmly in the nave, one thing
she never spoke of was her fear of
going bald, wearing an enormous hat.
She had a heart for Albania,
raising money and sending hand or
treadle sewing machines, thus granting
economic independence to the girls.
She collected used stamps in the same cause,
for which the Dean had, so he was told,
agreed to site a box in the back pew.
We always knew where we stood with Primrose.
Listening to her was a litany
of who was in the good books of the Lord.
One day she called me for a consignment
in one of her operations, we went
direct to the depot where, by sheer force
of will, the *Officially Had To Be
Booked & Paid For Online Only* package—
was accepted on paper for cash.
She wasn't one for women priests, but took
an Orthodox stance. Of all the saints
she reminds me of Monica, arriving
at her son, Augustine's consecration
the only one to come (in the City
the custom had long since fallen out of use)
with an agápé basket. She's gone now,
passed. Somewhere in heaven there's a new
collecting box for used prayers
to be recycled for Albania.

## St Stephen's Eve

I'm watching one of those films, the plot
starts with, Will they get it on or not?
He is Jude Law; she, I don't know who,
is (in the film) *Alice,* one of two
female leads, the other's Julia
what's-her-name. They work themselves into
conventional snafutizations, and
of course they do, get it on, that is.
but not on screen which is a relief.
It's much more serious. I don't desire
to watch them pretending to have sex, I care
about them more than that, these kinds
of people who, like us at the movies,
come to happy endings, everyone
getting to go home. They might act hurt, feel
life's not worth living any more, despair
of ever getting it together.
If only it were really like that, it would
all be so much simpler. Nowadays
I count the grief. Every year there's three days
coming round of death: on Christmas day
the girl I first loved many years ago,
before I met & knew my late wife;
who's lying in a field, though whether
she's watching or counting sheep, I don't know;
and of course the day I get there too:
It's like a birthday but we don't know when.
Whatever. In the end, it'll be like
Christmas. Angels rousing us from sleep.

## LUGETE O VENERES CUPIDINESQUE

time to get grieving my beauties,
hetero, gay, or bi: my birdie,
my bird's little sparrow, is dead,
that cutey sparrow, that darling
bird, brighter than her own bright eye;
that little tweetie-pie, he got
closer to her than a girl gets
close to her mummykins, to her alone
while he lived in her lap, hop hand to hand
left right up down cheep-cheep cheep-cheep:
my birdie's taken a one-way flight-
ticket to deep deep thicketest shade.
Death, I wish you the worst I can
wasting my bird her pretty man:
you've snatched such a beauty from me,
poor birdie, poor wicked wee thing:
it's you that's made my birdie's bright bright eyes
get rubbed all red with weep, weep, weep.

## QUIS MULTA GRACILIS

Hej! what lithe and rosy fingered lad
busting to give you one, now have you got
up your sea-nymph grotto? For whose
eye do you gather, ginger floss, your gold

tresses so simply? Truly he, poor chap,
is in for a rough ride, imagining
he'll master you with his single oar.
Little he knows the moment of your

tiny rudder, or what urgent storms
he's in for before you skip & jump ship.
He thinks you'll always part waves for him,
be always his sunshine! How I feel his pain.

Yet don't concern yourself with me. Here I,
your jettisoned Crusoe, made it to the shore.
Wet through, cleaned out, hung out to dry,
I count my blessings. Jotting these poor thanks.

## LOCKDOWN SPRING

My sister sends me unwritten
a picture postcard, post-war, colour,
*The Source of the Thames.*
A pool surrounded by pink stone
from which runs a rivulet.
Is this the only begetter
of Mother Isis, Father Thames?
She says we were taken there by ours
when she was three and remembers
or alleges she does. I was two
and have no memory, until
perhaps now this imprint. Maybe
it is the Type, of what I call *The Pool
of Silence* in my mind, the place between
the worlds where I can go & plunge in,
can bathe in the reincarnational
waters' clarity.  But here, there's more:
Railed off, as if for all the world it were
one of those self-important parish
graveyard tombs, is the reclining figure,
trident in hand, of the presiding god.
The flow of waters is wisely
protected from his management.
Even after threescore years and ten
not to be trusted with the innocent.

## MUDFLATS

In a downstream corner of the mudflats
there's a wreck. When first I came here twenty
five, six years ago, it was whole, for sale,
a little bit run down, certainly, but
lived in, they said, although nothing's certain.
That's how she presented, and there were signs,
the gang plank with the light chain stretched across.
The story was she was a Kirkwall Drifter,
one of the last wooden hulls laid down
1920 or a few years later.
She maintained a presence, a certain
status as a fixture and she was,
or became, how these things happen, the cause
is often obscure, uncertain, contested,
derelict. The sole if it was her sole
crew found dead aboard of an overdose.
She started to lose the gold first, or rather
more simply the yellow. The black paint
peeled to reveal black timbers. She settled
lying on one side naked like Goya's
Duchess on her chaise longue. Her decking, slats,
strakes, coaxed open piece by piece to let
light in where ought to be the dark, and no
light matter to expose what ought to be
private, a matter of warmly chambered
purpose, not this tidal ravishing
quotidian beauty of daylight. She's
there still, at the turn of the day's tide
or the night's, on the downstream mudflats.

## At a First Meeting

New Pigeon to Old Timer,
How do I get this thing?

You want to Stop?
Whatever it takes?

Yes, I want it,
I'll do anything.

Good. Don't drink,
Don't think, Go to meetings.

What does it mean
Don't think?

It means, Don't ask questions,
don't argue, just do it.

Surely it can't
be that simple?

Listen: I'll be here
tomorrow night

and for all I know
you might be right.

## CHOCOLATE MOUSSE

I used to be a devil for the girls:
one on the go, one on the way out,
one on the slipway ready. -I come
from a long & salty line of seafarers:
Sledge out the chocks, heave, tip, lightly,
lightly, till she... dips her head and
go, sprint, sprint! Reach out, steady and
jump! Boom-boom go the metal rollers, swish
goes the reach and the gentle draw
of the salt & pulse of the all-accepting,
nameless and seedless sea.

It was a balancing act,
more act than balancing: I forget -
but even if I didn't,
it'd be- *No Names No Pack Drill!*
How was it for me?
Sometimes on changeover day
hand in hand on the echoing strand
it was as if we belonged together, we,
we'd go out together, she and me,
one of the three. These days I'm alone,
I sit on the sofa, eating chocolate mousse,
Tesco's finest two for one,
tastes best with a long spoon.

## REMEMBRANCE DAY AT PLAYING PLACE

Five minutes to eleven precisely
We form up in rough twos into the yard.
At the front there's talking indistinctly.
Voices are tired. Cold. Hungry. Lonely. Scared.

The children march between us as we stand.
We know the truth. Their silence dutiful.
Smiling they glance about. We had not planned
That they would always be so beautiful.

Can this grey light be daylight or is this
Pretence of light to serve in place of light?
We don't know what there is, which makes it worse,
To be afraid of. Here. It's getting late.

The man at the front falls silent. As if
These prayers are heard. If not by me then who?
I am not listening. It is not safe
To know too much, or hope.

Living as yet, upright, remembering
These dead of all our wars, we stand our ground.
In certain hope of the resurrection.
All for our comfort to this certain end.

And of a sudden, in this nameless yard,
These bare trees standing guard on us in grey,
The long-awaited trumpet sound is heard
And nothing. We break up no ground this day.

Yet here, our breathing bodies simply turn
To air and shadow. We begin to sink
Into the earth: over our ankles, knees,
Thighs, up to the waist, and still descending.

Earth without a murmur is accepting
Us (you too belong here) that have no cause
To fear our future, nor the heat of the sun,
Nor the moon's blight, nor her inconstant laws.

I tell you this is how it was. The most
Strange thing. I tell you simply what I saw
And heard and did. Or rather what my ghost
(Poor Ghost!) made of these notes.

                    These notes. No more.

## ANSWER TO A COMPLAINT THAT MY POEMS ARE TOO...

all i have to do to stay alive
is keep breathing
yes, that's all
all i have to do
all i have
to do, yes

Living is a good thing
walking in the light
and then it's time to
when it's time to
sleep and we are
for the dark

## DIFFICULT

when all's said & done I try to
keep it very simple
plain, straightforward
no arcane
classical references

or, if there are,
buried so deep
no-one is troubled by
missing them, or feels
defeated by irrelevant
rhetorical scholarship

like General Patton's front-line
encouragement, bawling out:
*Come on you guys, anyone'd think*
*you wanted to live for ever!*

        and how many recognise, or know
        he's quoting Cicero?

## THE FULL PICTURE

Life's in the end something of a jigsaw.
Only you don't get the picture, the box
is broken, there's no simple exchanging
this one for that one, you can never be
sure you've got all the pieces or how many
there are supposed to be. So far so simple.
What first you set aside for the edges
turn out to be anything but, and colours
might be patched black whitey yellow & brown,
or all mixed up in a dazzle of flags
at the running river bank's vexatious
or welcome meanderments. 'Til when at last
a picture (which is absolutely nothing
like what's not on the box) begins to emerge
you find that the corners are all in
the middle, full stop. And you never quite know
how the pieces or the picture really fits,
but only your neighbour can tell you.
Except I've noticed some of the most
beautiful pieces of missing are still
in my hand but only when it's in yours.
And I give you my word, even if I have
to reach into the dark to touch you,
what I have to do is almost done.
And your jigsaw, which when you left it was
such an unfinished mess, in unsorted
piles of pieces from assorted puzzles,
has resolved into a clearer picture.
Not *A cottage in a wood by a stream*
but, full of light and, here's what's amazing!
angels somehow, full of light and peace.

## Words for Young Lovers

In the communion of saints
the dead get together,
but have no fleshy parts
with which to make pleasure.

Their bones get mixed,
like Frideswide & the Dean's wife
make common sainthood
out of red blood & blue.

The most in this life we can do
is be our selves, completely
in gift to one whose receiving
is their same gift to us too.

It seems so simple,
all that anyone can do.

If you truly believe that
I've got news for you:

any one
but not any two.

## CYTHEREAN ENCOUNTER

If I were to tell you that tomorrow
some time, I don't exactly know when,
the Earth, he said, will be struck by a rock
the size of Cyprus –Cyprus, she said,
I was born in Cyprus! –So I have cause,
he said, to believe. So beautiful an island,
but this island, this heavenly body
will punch a hole through Earth's crust
leaving the Yellowstone caldera
looking like a party popper. So,
(he stood right close to her) all the world
will end in terror, fire, the sun
set fast in everlasting night.
Would you? Knowing we are all
about to die? He looked her in the eye:
It is sudden, he said. We are all there is,
We are only tonight. But how do I tell,
she said, the summer lightening in her eyes,
that what you know is true? And if I fall
into your arms, and if our passion makes
all the world anew, what then? What if
there's no asteroid impact, no end
of the world and it carries on bravely?
And all this a credulous ploy to lie
your way into my bed? You'll know the truth
he said, when you feel... When I feel? –she arched
an eyebrow. When you feel the earth move, he said.

## BLIND DATE

She really wowed the studio with her red cloak.
No way was she visiting her boring old granny.
She asked what food they' d have her with, and why;
And number one with the wicked smile
Said, "Pick me, Darling, I'll have you
For a hot lunch!" -and to cheers she did.

And at the end of the week,
To show she had not really been eaten,
The girl now truly scarlet came right back
Hand in hand with the Big Bad Wolf;
The widest of smiles on their faces
As safely friends as any child could wish.

Only a few in the audience, almost
None of the viewers, out there in the world,
Saw the red floss between the huge white teeth;
Or the thin sewn line, drawn like red marker pen
Round the girl's slim neck; or·suspected
The body-heat of her warm, synchronized grin.

## SWANS

I have done nothing unusual:
kept a dog; got my children;
fallen in love, with the emphasis
on fallen - did I ever tell you how,
after I went to the vets,
I discovered, at 48,
the novel experience
of thinking with my brain?
sobered up from my first full-time
career as a drunk; practised,
but without much financial success,
unremarkable small-town law.

And today the tenth anniversary
of my father's death. Had we
been friends, had I felt
that he cared about me at all,
life might have been different
for him as well as for me,
our failures, successes, burdens.
His life was his will: in contrast, mine
has traced the rivers of the underworld,
stood in the margins of twilight, watched
events unfold in white and black.

Like swans.

## TERRACOTTA

Mother had brown eyes, Father blue,
the colour of sky before sunrise.

Hers I recall clearly, his
are more distant, cloudier days.

One day I picked up and carelessly broke
a little Spanish dish, the kind they make

to sell to tourists as they pass,
grey slip painted blue-green glaze.

There was pain in her eyes and anger,
more when I said it didn't matter.

Now I'm as old as she was then
washing my own small dish from Spain.

They had bought it together
before he ran out on her,

a link back to a whole
world before that fall:

that small, glazed dish, which
I had not, till I broke it, noticed.

Blue shards dumped in the bin.
I've carried them fifty years since then.

Those sharp-edged, brown-sided pieces.
Those wet, terracotta eyes.

## READING TO THE BEAR

1.  The Gospel


I am standing in my living room
reading to my teddy-bear.
Not the bear that is here
but the bear that is over there.

I have chosen the largest available
room & as instructed place the audience
at the other end, taking my stance
in the light. In order

to be seen, to be heard, to be clear.
Let it be simply every word.
Be slow. If you think it too
slow, be slower, slower, until

it really is, then cut the pauses.
Put in the ends of the lines.
Project the voice. Not with a shout
but let the volume be complete.

Like in the Gospel when his friend is sick,
they send urgently for him to come.
He gets the text and waits a day or three
until at last he turns up but too late.

If you had been here, sir,
my brother had not died.
And if I had, what then?
The verse is, Jesus wept. We get

the rest of the tale. If we open up
the tomb, sir, it'll be a health-hazard.
We'll need an exhumation licence.
All the usual bureaucratic guff.

At which the Lord says simply Open it.
And then he stands there. Like I'd like to,
reading *The Raising* one Cathedral Sunday,
let'm wait a pause or three, until

here's the moment for the voice in full
to lift through all the vault, the tall
pillars & ribs, the battle-flags in the aisles,
the tongue of the altar-cloth, the cassocked quire

adozing in their double-tiered rows,
the Dean & his assistants, looking
puzzled at one another, wondering
What's up with Robinson now?

Has he lost his place, lost his voice,
had a seizure? What on earth? And that's
the moment I'd just like to take
the text by the throat and, turning off the mike,

let my voice fill all that corbelled vault
with, *Lazrus! Come Forth*! But all
I am is standing in a poem here,
reading to my teddy-bear.


   2.   The Soliloquy


Not the bear that is here,
but the bear that is over there.
The bear that is bald, that is hard
of hearing, stiff in the joints,

worn thin in flank and thigh,
no longer silken-soft of fur,
the bear that is missing an eye,
the bear whose critical ear

demands my every simple word.
How can I know what the poem
is, unless I plainly hear
what each word does, and each pause?

I used to be at the front, I used
to be my maker's constant toy,
I was the bear who comforted
and kept amused, and shared the spoken

and unspoken childish joys
and sorrows of my learning boy:
I was the bear and I am the bear
though I sit at the back in a special chair

that used to be and was always there.
All through the rehearsals I was the bear
that listened and heard and had time to spare
and never got tired whatever was shared

and even when the stuff I heard
was inarticulate raw pain
I would drink it in, until the word
comes to burst it forth again

and then I bring it to the light
unwrap this dreadful buried thing
afraid of the stink and the heaving white
corruption such uncovering

might reveal on its return until at last
in the silence here, there's nothing more
to say or do. Nothing to fear
in the listening gaze of the faithful bear.

## I HAVE NOT SLEPT SOUNDLY

They say it is unlucky
to let the moon shine in aslant
through glass or an open window
onto where you are sleeping.

Yet when you catch moonrise
think of me. I am part of you.
It cannot be unlucky
for me to look at you

whether your face sleeping
or all of you in the nakedness
of moon-glow on your skin.
So when you read this

remember, summer moonlight
once, and me sleeping.
You woke me tenderly.
I have not slept soundly since.

Let the moon fill your house
as completely as it can;
a faithful lover, quieter
than shadow visiting.

I have gone far to forget you
but it is no use. I come back
always to where we start from
because I take my self.

Reaching my destination
when I get there I find you;
through travail & labour
the truth is I never left.

And if we were to meet
now in this life, my body,
your body, somewhere banal
the station the dock the airport

heaven knows what I would do.
Stand there and weep I guess.
Hold you in silence. What
could be said would not be this.

## CARRYING THE TORCH, 20ᵀᴴ MARCH, 2022

*Thomas Cranmer, tried in St Mary's, High St, Oxford;*
*burnt outside the Northgate, 21 March 1556*

This unequal midnight I walk through
from the High, down Catte Street, past the Bod
& along the Broad, seeking the stone cross
layered in the tarmac opposite Oxfam.

In the small hours it can be not unsafe
to stand here. Once I even knelt.
Shutting out the streetlight you can hear
the flinch of doubt, the crack of thorn & flame.

For all our prayer for peace, our nature
does not change. The same opportune
power tempts. What can I say, this night
of Putin's war? The barbarians

at the gate are always us. Thomas,
our burnt Archbishop, pray for us. Help us
to trust your doubt, your faltered faith.
Help us stretch our hand into the fire.

## SAN ROMANO

Am I the single person in the world
who passing a skip in the road just wants
to sort it all, the wood, the boxes, old
door furniture to salvage even if bent?

Like in the supermarket. The woman
next to me's shopping's always much more
interesting. What's she got at home
to buy all that peculiar lot for?

Sometimes I remark on it. Well, I say,
clearly you're a lover of cats; or, What
a bundle of [whatever]. - It's a way
of breaking the ice. Less often than not.

Though sometimes I recall my old girlfriend
Lizzie that married Alan & did Art
in Academia. We'd correspond
from school to school, apart but heart to heart.

And one day (this she wrote) at the National
by Trafalgar Square, a man she'd never
met nor did again, by the great panel
of *San Romano* asked If she'd ever

(he must have been awfully lonely) Thought
of getting, um, er, what's the word, yes, Please
Would you Marry me? O Please? How she fought
back tears of laughter in the telling, "He's

probably unspeakably mad, so
I, as kindly as I could, made an
excuse and left".  She left so long ago.
I wonder what became, though, of the man?

## CLOSE INCIDENT

A man who had fallen upon hard times
was sleeping rough under the Chapter House.
I took care to step round him, coming down
early this morning to Morning Prayer. He was
invisible, buried in a white mound
of sleeping bag & blankets on the bricked,
concreted common ground of the car park.
Sleeping soundly, a pair of crossed crutches
within reach at the head of his exclusive,
provisional & narrow, space & bound.
    When I came out he was back on his feet
standing with one foot in his sleeping bag.
I asked him, *You alright*? He said, *Please help,
my hip is broken, I got beaten up,
I can't lift my leg to get my foot off
to pack up my bag.* I helped as best I could
untangle his dead foot from the white cloth.
    With a suspect thought of taking him home
or giving him a lift to [wherever]
I asked him, *Do you want something to eat*?
He said, *I need the toilet.* I knew
there's one in the Cathedral, but thought
he'd never with that leg make the steps
up to the Cloister door, and even if
he could, this early on Sundays they're still locked.
Besides, I hadn't time to speak before
he said, *I've got to do a Number Two,
right now!* and turned away, *You don't*, he said,
*want to watch.* So I went to the car.
    Last sight of him was with his back to me
and his bag between us, as he fumbled
urgently with his belt. And he was right:
shitting in The Close is not my scene.
    I'm not sure of my ministry to him,
but his to me is certain. Once again, I'm
one that passes by still, on the other side.

## PASSENGERS

66 million years ago, a rock
the size of Sark, punched through the earth's crust
at Yucatan, thus precipitating
the closure of Jurassic Park. It took
five million years to get the lights back on.
Summer & winter, cold & heat, sunrise
and sunset, seedtime & harvest – everything
back to evolutionary normal.
The smaller mammals were doing OK
until some clever dick, perhaps wanting
to see further than was good for him,
tried running on two legs. "Here I am,
*hominid sum*, the first of humankind
by which I am entitled to style
myself *Sapiens*, a natural improvement
on the last dispensation. I am aware
of my own awareness, which no other
creature is. (This appears ignorant
of recent work with elephant, dolphin,
and corvid self-recognition. Ed.) I am
the apex and the end of all that our
designer God has purposed." I'm not sure
how to respond to this. Perhaps a meek
mention of the fact that Grandma, telling me
in 1963, about her visit
to New York in '89, very much—
from how she smacked her lips with relish—
enjoyed her dinner of passenger pigeon.

## At Vespers

In the woods when we were children we found
a ruined cabin about a mile from home
along the main road, turn right down the lane,
left where the fallen tree-stump lifts the ground
in a great arch of trailing roots & pale earth
dry to creep under and through, at the edge
of the wood, secretly, out from the public
cover of the sky, unseen from the road.
There was no path to it, it simply stood.

  The window-frames were metal, so it can't
have been older than before the War.
But the glass was gone and red oxide bars
broke up the black of the blank interior.
It stood completely in the trees, around it
no clearing, no function, or if ever
it had one, none we could discover.

We never explored inside the cabin,

although well old enough and had the makeshift skill,

to make it into a den or place to go.

It stood there in the wood, just off the lane.

Over the years I have wondered again

on occasion to visit, and take alone

the trouble to be there in the bluebell wood

and find the cabin standing, if not as

it is, then as it was, and if I should

re-enter there the minding of a child.

## WOLF AT NEW MOON

Wolf had a human wife once. Her legs
as smooth as ash, her body as bright
in movement as aspen in sunlight,
her eyes as hard to paint as the laughter
of a stream. She would hold him potent
in her gaze with wonder and stillness.
This was not always sexual, but was
a more than simply physical event.
He would lower his weight onto the splay
of his wide paws and hold there panting.
She would watch him as he, never
taking his eyes off her, reduced
his body to her ground, his black nose
resting at last on her feet. Others
who met him, met only his human form,
assumed he had no other shape than this.
When they were alone, she knew him
only ever as wolf. When they slept
together she would scrunch his neck, his back,
stretching her dreams to the limit;
he tireless and without cease running
through shadows of starlight, through all
the promise and pregnancy of her,
her reassurance she would constantly
hunt him down, her white and red
unfailing iterations of the moon.

## THIS NIGHT

I dreamt of oysters

They were singing
Light centred all around us
All that is left is wonder
But in my dream, I knew
If only I could remember
it would be clear

These words are so wooden
a clunky pile of cardboard boxes
constructed by a child, a pretend car,
magic carpet, a sailing or a spaceship
in default of the real thing
they're a pile of rubbish

But to get back to the oysters
the flat shells are the wheels
rainbows of light
the hollow shells are cups
a scoop of wine barely touches
the lip, is a breath of...
and yet it does not burn

I wake tasting salt

## PROSECUTION EXHIBIT ##

We have rebuilt the towers. In hope
to have accommodation ready
for your arrival. Until then, these
lines are idle. Indeed, apart from
this idleness we live a normal life.
Construction. All things considered
we are making good progress. Our needs:
materials of all and special
kinds; industrial chemicals bricks
cement lime timber steel ceramics
wire; most gauges of pipe, for liquids
and of course gas. Personnel. Discreet
lists compiling. We have considered
air transport, but on balance the rail
connection is still best. All we know
how well it proved its value, lasting
continuous use throughout the most
enormous difficulties.

And now,

with this pause — they're almost forgotten,

it is so long since last the fat smoke

bloomed at these stacks. And we have taken

time quietly to improve throughput.

Speed. Administration. Each unit

on arrival to be implanted

with a chip, for scanning and update

at each stage of the process. As well

as avoiding error, it means less

risk, as was the case with paper, of

scrutiny in hands which do not share

necessity in truth as all we

do. And finally, not only have

we eliminated from the smoke

all odour, so that our location

can maintain discretion, and our plant

centralize its own convenient

gross productive population, but

the implant chip itself is fully

biodegradable.

## Bringing in the Washing

I've an odd sock.

How can it be an odd sock
unless we have the other which
it does not match? by itself
there's nothing that makes it odd.

It's the same with people:
if they're a true pair
how does one know which is which?
And if they don't match
conventional wisdom says
they're not a pair.

We made up a pair although
one could always tell us apart,
we were a match that didn't match
she was one I was the other
together we made up, for a while,
a simple and apparent whole.

This is all I have left.
People who aren't used to me
ask sometimes *Why do you wear odd socks?*
Listen... if today I'm wearing
two socks and I've got one on each foot
I reckon I'm doing pretty well

Although, some days
I still check the washing line
to see if by some impossibly odd
miracle the one I'm missing
is still hanging out.

## ALCOHOLIC INCIDENT

But, she said, and this is the hard bit, not
since I was 15 and my mother put
herself first and me into care. Which is how
and the whole trip, beginning as a child.
Now I've got money and, to work from,
my own flat but no-where to live. Then, once
when I was a student. Then, not again
until, four months ago, I needed, to
find out who I am. And know who he is.

And now you know, I said, he is the kind
of man who is an alcoholic and
who- But, she said, my mother said she warned
me not to, but, he told me he didn't,
and he kept saying all the time we were,
believe, she said, he is my father and,
You're not getting any of my, he said,
a tart like you, money. And, No, she said,
he didn't give me any. It wasn't
like that. Not him. Just got me drunk instead.

## NORTH,
Ottawa to Vancouver, via Marathon

Do you remember driving across?
We stopped near dawn at a lay-by,
our two little girls in the back
always looking out for the School Bus.

Bus! they'd shout, Bus! Full of childish excitement,
keen to see and play with their cousins,
not comprehending all we'd left behind,
you sister and her people, as we headed west.

In that morning quiet, the engine
stilled in the stillness of the white dew,
the prairie infinite around us,

we heard in the high,
far distance of the plain,
the working faint honk-honk of the geese.
We looked up, there they were, in sunlight,

a mile perhaps above our shadow,
hard to say, the clear vee of arctic geese
in May migration north,
the  green warmth of their summer home.

This was years ago. Our daughters are grown,
and we are growing, if not already grown, old.
yet I have never forgotten the crossing of our path
in this dark life by the geese, with their simple

certainty of summer in the north.
That all is well. That's all.
Not long now I too will be heading North

# NOTES

**In Personam** lit "in a persona".

A persona is a mask to present a character in a functional role. We commonly present personae in our various adult roles in life: student, parent, lover, job/ profession, member of [X], prophet, healer, storyteller, politician, hooligan, etc. While a poem might be composed/written by the poet, it is not (or is not always or automatically or simply) the author that is the speaker, the voice of utterance of the poem.

These might initially present as simple & private soliloquies, until you begin to reckon the people present: the character speaking  the poem, the person/s they address, you the reader/ audience, the author, the person the author intends the poem for, etc.

In this book, some of the voices of utterance are male, some not; some are almost, like Swans, me; most but not all live in a world that recognizably resembles our own (but where, at what age? date? present/past/future? [on which planet?]).

As a student I probably read more of Browning, especially *Men & Women* than was good for me; and perhaps not [yet] enough Cavafy.

**passim** If in places the punctuation, and the grammar (such as it is) seems difficult, please forgive me, it is transcription of speech, which works differently.

**Lockdown Spring**     the source of the Thames (more precisely the Isis) has been reconfigured and is no longer as presented in the referenced picture-postcard photograph.

**Remembrance Day at Playing Place**

Playing Place, TR3 is served by St Kea Church.  As recorded in the footnote, these lines transcribe contemporaneous notes of a vision. The Last Post ending the two minutes silence is sounded on a bugle rather than a trumpet, which technical inaccuracy in the poem has purpose; as might well also have the echoes of the plays.

**Answer to a complaint . . .**
See the note for *Remembrance Day*, and elsewhere passim: most of the quasi-quotations, misquotations, echoes, and borrowings are intentional.

**. . . difficult**
apologies, I cannot find my recorded reference or source for the quote, which accordingly appears (as is not uncommon) to be invented.

**Words for Young Lovers**
When the Cathedral shrine of St Frideswide (her name means *Bond of Peace*), patron of Oxford was despoiled in the protestant reformation, her casket was re-used for the remains of the Dean's wife; but when under Mary Tudor the Roman rite was restored and the Saint's bones were retranslated to their proper home, the two sets of earthly remains became, somehow, inextricably intermixed.

**Cytherean Encounter**
his odious, chauvinistic egocentricity is ignorant & careless of the fact that the earth as a habitable entity would hardly survive impact of so large an asteroid

**Carrying the Torch**
a *layer* is a flat-laid monument, flush with the floor or ground; the Oxfam shop is at 17 Broad St.

**Passengers**    *Ectopistes migratorius.*

**At Vespers**    north of Bagley Wood lane, nearer the Chandlings (or top) end.

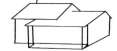

*Website: www.hovelpress.co.uk*

The Hovel Press publishes the following titles:

*For Young Adults:*

| | |
|---|---|
| Seiriol's Quest | 2016 |
| Cornish Bits and Pieces | 2021 |
| Terrible Tales | 2022 |

*Poetry:*

| | |
|---|---|
| Possibly Mabe | 2014 |
| Looking Out | 2016 |
| From the Chellew Room | 2016 |
| Uneasy Heads | 2021 |
| In Personam | 2022 |
| Landmarks | 2022 |